EXTRACT FROM A LETTER IN "MISCELLANEOUS WRITINGS"

By Mary Baker Eddy

The Rules and By-laws in the Manual of The First Church of Christ, Scientist, Boston, originated not in solemn conclave as in ancient Sanhedrim. They were not arbitrary opinions nor dictatorial demands, such as one person might impose on another. They were impelled by a power not one's own, were written at different dates, and as the occasion required. They sprang from necessity, the logic of events,—from the immediate demand for them as a help that must be supplied to maintain the dignity and defense of our Cause; hence their simple, scientific basis, and detail so requisite to demonstrate genuine Christian Science, and which will do for the race what absolute doctrines destined for future generations might not accomplish.

TENETS

of The Mother Church

The First Church of Christ, Scientist

To be signed by those uniting with The First Church of Christ, Scientist, in Boston, Mass.

1. As adherents of Truth, we take the inspired Word of the Bible as our sufficient guide to eternal Life.

2. We acknowledge and adore one supreme and infinite God. We acknowledge His Son, one Christ; the Holy Ghost or divine Comforter; and man in God's image and likeness.

3. We acknowledge God's forgiveness of sin in the destruction of sin and the spiritual understanding that casts out evil as unreal. But the belief in sin is punished so long as the belief lasts.

4. We acknowledge Jesus' atonement as the evidence of divine, efficacious Love, unfolding man's unity with God through Christ Jesus the Way-shower; and we acknowledge that man is saved through Christ, through Truth, Life, and Love as demonstrated by the Galilean Prophet in healing the sick and overcoming sin and death.

5. We acknowledge that the crucifixion of Jesus and his resurrection served to uplift faith to understand eternal Life, even the allness of Soul, Spirit, and the nothingness of matter.

6. And we solemnly promise to watch, and pray for that Mind to be in us which was also in Christ Jesus; to do unto others as we would have them do unto us; and to be merciful, just, and pure.

MARY BAKER EDDY

HISTORICAL SKETCH

In the spring of 1879, a little band of earnest seekers after Truth went into deliberations over forming a church without creeds, to be called the "CHURCH OF CHRIST, SCIENTIST." They were members of evangelical churches, and students of Mrs. Mary Baker Eddy in Christian Science, and were known as "Christian Scientists."

At a meeting of the Christian Scientist Association, April 12, 1879, on motion of Mrs. Eddy, it was voted,—To organize a church designed to commemorate the word and works of our Master, which should reinstate primitive Christianity and its lost element of healing.

Mrs. Eddy was appointed on the committee to draft the Tenets of the Mother Church—the chief corner stone whereof is, that Christian Science, as taught and demonstrated by our Master, casts out error, heals the sick, and restores the lost Israel: for "the stone which the builders rejected, the same is become the head of the corner."

The charter for the Church was obtained June, 1879,[1] and the same month the members, twenty-six in number, extended a call to Mary Baker Eddy to become their pastor. She accepted the call, and was ordained A. D. 1881. Although walking through deep waters, the little Church went steadily on, increasing in numbers, and at every epoch saying,

"Hitherto hath the Lord helped us."

On the twenty-third day of September, 1892, at the request of Rev. Mary Baker Eddy, twelve of her students and Church members met and reorganized, under her jurisdiction, the Christian Science Church and named it, THE FIRST CHURCH OF CHRIST, SCIENTIST.

At this meeting twenty others of Mrs. Eddy's students and members of her former Church were elected members of this Church,—those with others that have since been elected were known as "First Members." The Church Tenets, Rules, and By-Laws, as prepared by Mrs. Eddy, were adopted. A By-Law adopted March 17, 1903, changed the title of "First Members" to "Executive Members." (On July 8, 1908, the By-Laws pertaining to "Executive Members" were repealed.)

THE FIRST CHURCH OF CHRIST, SCIENTIST, IN BOSTON, MASS., is designed to be built on the Rock, Christ; even the understanding and demonstration of divine Truth, Life, and Love, healing and saving the world from sin and death; thus to reflect in some degree the Church Universal and Triumphant.

[1] Steps were taken to promote the Church of Christ, Scientist, in April, May and June; formal organization was accomplished and the charter obtained in August, 1879.

CHURCH OFFICERS

Rev. MARY BAKER EDDY Pastor Emeritus

GEORGE WENDELL ADAMS Christian Science Board of Directors

CHARLES E. HEITMAN

Mrs. NELVIA E. RITCHIE

FRANCIS LYSTER JANDRON

ALFRED PITTMAN

Mrs. HELEN CHAFFEE ELWELL President

THOMAS E. HURLEY First Reader

Conducts services and reads from

the Christian Science textbook,

"SCIENCE AND HEALTH WITH KEY TO THE

SCRIPTURES" by Mary Baker Eddy

Mrs. GEORGINA TENNANT Second Reader

Reads from the SCRIPTURES

GORDON V. COMER Clerk, 107 Falmouth Street, Boston, Mass.

ROY GARRETT WATSON Treasurer, 107 Falmouth Street, Boston, Mass. 1947-1948

CHURCH BY-LAWS

CHURCH OFFICERS

Article I—NAMES, ELECTION, AND DUTIES

Names. SECTION 1. The Church officers shall consist of the Pastor Emeritus, a Board of Directors, a President, a Clerk, a Treasurer, and two Readers.

President. SECTION 2. The President shall be elected, subject to the approval of the Pastor Emeritus, by the Board of Directors[2] on Monday preceding the annual meeting of the Church. The President shall hold office for one year, and the same person is eligible for election but once in three years.

[2] See under "Deed of Trust" for incorporation of the "Christian Science Board of Directors."

Clerk and Treasurer. SECTION 3. The term of office for the Clerk and the Treasurer of this Church (also for the editors and the manager of The Christian Science Publishing Society, and the manager of the general Committee on Publication in Boston) is one year each, dating from the time of election to office. Incumbents who have served one year or more, may be re-elected, or new officers elected, at the annual meeting held for this purpose, by a unanimous vote of the Christian Science Board of Directors and the consent of the Pastor Emeritus given in her own handwriting.

Readers. SECTION 4. Every third year Readers shall be elected in The Mother Church by the Board of Directors, which shall inform the Pastor Emeritus of the names of its candidates before they are elected; and if she objects, said candidates shall not be chosen.

The Directors shall fix the salaries of the Readers.

Directors. SECTION 5. The Christian Science Board of Directors shall consist of five members. They shall fill a vacancy occurring on that Board after the candidate is approved by the Pastor Emeritus. A majority vote or the request of Mrs. Eddy shall dismiss a member. Members shall neither report the discussions of this Board, nor those with Mrs. Eddy.

Church Business. SECTION 6. The business of The Mother Church shall be transacted by its Christian Science Board of Directors. The manager of the general Committee on Publication in the United States shall order no special action to be taken by said Committee that is not named in the Manual of this Church without consulting with the full Board of Directors of The Mother Church and receiving the written consent of said Board.

Publishing Buildings. SECTION 7. It shall be the duty of the Christian Science Board of Directors to provide a suitable building for the publication of The Christian Science Journal, Christian Science Sentinel, Der Herold der Christian Science, and all other Christian Science literature published by The Christian Science Publishing Society. It shall also be the duty of the Christian Science Board of Directors to provide suitable rooms, conveniently and pleasantly located in the same building, for the publication and sale of the books of which Mary Baker Eddy is, or may be, the author, and of other literature connected therewith.

Trusteeships and Syndicates. SECTION 8. Boards of Trustees and Syndicates may be formed by The Mother Church, subject to the approval of the Pastor Emeritus.

Duties of Church Officers. SECTION 9. Law constitutes government, and disobedience to the laws of The Mother Church must ultimate in annulling its Tenets and By-Laws. Without a proper system of government and form of action, nations, individuals, and religion are unprotected; hence the necessity of this By-Law and the warning of Holy Writ: "That servant, which knew his lord's will, and prepared not himself, neither did according to his will, shall be beaten with many stripes."

It is the duty of the Christian Science Board of Directors to watch and make sure that the officers of this Church perform the functions of their several offices promptly and well. If an officer fails to fulfil all the obligations of his office, the Board of Directors shall immediately call a meeting and notify this officer either to resign his place or to perform his office faithfully; then failing to do either, said officer shall be dismissed from this Church, and his dismissal shall be written on the Church records.

It is the duty of any member of this Church, and especially of one who has been or who is the First Reader of a church, to inform the Board of Directors of the failure of the Committee on Publication or of any other officer in this Church to perform his official duties. A Director shall not make known the name of the complainant.

If the Christian Science Board of Directors fails to fulfil the requirements of this By-Law, and a member of this Church or the Pastor Emeritus shall complain thereof to the Clerk and the complaint be found valid, the Directors shall resign their office or perform their functions faithfully. Failing to do thus, the Pastor Emeritus shall appoint five suitable members of this Church to fill the vacancy. The salary of the members of the Board of Directors shall be at present two thousand five hundred dollars each annually.

Article II—READERS OF THE MOTHER CHURCH

Election. SECTION 1. The Readers for The Mother Church shall be a man and a woman, one to read the BIBLE, and one to read SCIENCE AND HEALTH WITH KEY TO THE SCRIPTURES.

Eligibility. SECTION 2. The Directors shall select intelligible

Readers who are exemplary Christians and good English scholars.

They must be members of The Mother Church.

Removal. SECTION 3. If a Reader in The Mother Church be found at any time inadequate or unworthy, he or she shall be removed from office by a majority vote of the Board of Directors and the consent of the Pastor Emeritus, and the vacancy supplied.

First Reader's Residence. SECTION 4. Unless Mrs. Eddy requests otherwise, the First Reader of The Mother Church shall occupy, during his term of Readership, the house of the Pastor Emeritus, No. 385 Commonwealth Avenue, Boston. The Board of Directors shall pay from the Church funds the taxes and rent on this property; the Board shall attend to the insurance before it expires, suitably furnish the house, and keep the property in good repair, so long as Mrs. Eddy does not occupy the house herself and the occupants are satisfactory to her.

Article III—DUTIES OF READERS OF THE MOTHER CHURCH AND OF ITS BRANCH CHURCHES

Moral Obligations. SECTION 1. The Readers of The Mother Church and of all its branch churches must devote a suitable portion of their time to preparation for the reading of the Sunday lesson,—a lesson on which the prosperity of Christian Science largely depends. They must keep themselves unspotted from the world,—uncontaminated with evil,—that the mental atmosphere they exhale shall promote health and holiness, even that spiritual animus so universally needed.

First Readers' Duties. SECTION 2. It shall be the duty of the First Readers to conduct the principal part of the Sunday services, and the Wednesday evening meetings.

Suitable Selections. SECTION 3. The First Readers shall read, as a part of the Wednesday evening services, selections from the SCRIPTURES, and from SCIENCE AND HEALTH WITH KEY TO THE SCRIPTURES.

Order of Reading. SECTION 4. The First Readers in the Christian Science churches shall read the correlative texts in SCIENCE AND HEALTH WITH KEY TO THE SCRIPTURES; and the Second Readers shall read the BIBLE texts. The readings from the SCRIPTURES shall precede the readings from SCIENCE AND HEALTH. The

Readers shall not read from copies or manuscripts, but from the books.

Naming Book and Author. SECTION 5. The Readers of SCIENCE AND HEALTH WITH KEY TO THE SCRIPTURES, before commencing to read from this book, shall distinctly announce the full title of the book and give the author's name. Such announcement shall be made but once during the lesson.

Readers in Branch Churches. SECTION 6. These Readers shall be members of The Mother Church. They shall read understandingly and be well educated. They shall make no remarks explanatory of the LESSON-SERMON at any time, but they shall read all notices and remarks that may be printed in the CHRISTIAN SCIENCE QUARTERLY. This By-Law applies to Readers in all the branch churches.

Enforcement of By-Laws. SECTION 7. It shall be the duty of every member of The Mother Church, who is a First Reader in a Church of Christ, Scientist, to enforce the discipline and by-laws of the church in which he is Reader.

A Reader not a Leader. SECTION 8. The Church Reader shall not be a Leader, but he shall maintain the Tenets, Rules, and discipline of the Church. A Reader shall not be a President of a church.

CHURCH MEMBERSHIP

Article IV—QUALIFICATIONS FOR MEMBERSHIP

Believe in Christian Science. SECTION 1. To become a
member of The Mother Church, the First Church of Christ,
Scientist, in Boston, Mass., the applicant must be a believer
in the doctrines of Christian Science, according to the
platform and teaching contained in the Christian Science
textbook, SCIENCE AND HEALTH WITH KEY TO THE
SCRIPTURES, by Rev. Mary Baker Eddy. The BIBLE,
together with SCIENCE AND HEALTH and other works
by Mrs. Eddy, shall be his only textbooks for self-
instruction in Christian Science, and for teaching and
practising metaphysical healing.

Free from Other Denominations. SECTION 2. This Church
will receive a member of another Church of Christ,
Scientist, but not a church member from a different
denomination until that membership is dissolved.

Children when Twelve Years Old. SECTION 3. Children
who have arrived at the age of twelve years, who are
approved, and whose applications are countersigned by one
of Mrs. Eddy's loyal students, by a Director, or by a student
of the Board of Education, may be admitted to membership
with The Mother Church.

Article V—APPLICATIONS FOR MEMBERSHIP

Students of the College. SECTION 1. Applications for
membership with The Mother Church from students of the
Massachusetts Metaphysical College who studied with

Rev. Mary Baker Eddy, shall be signed by the Christian Science Board of Directors as evidence of the loyalty of the applicants.

Other Students. SECTION 2. Applicants for membership who have not studied Christian Science with Rev. Mary Baker Eddy, can unite with this Church only by approval from students of Mrs. Eddy, loyal to the teachings of the textbook, SCIENCE AND HEALTH WITH KEY TO THE SCRIPTURES, or from members of The Mother Church, as provided in Article VI, Sect. 2, of these By-Laws.

Students' Pupils. SECTION 3. Applications for membership with The Mother Church, coming from pupils of loyal students who have taken the Primary or Normal Course at the Massachusetts Metaphysical College or in the Board of Education, or from pupils of those who have passed an examination by the Board of Education, shall have the approval and signature of their teachers, except in such cases as are provided for in Sect. 4 of this Article.

Exceptional Cases. SECTION 4. Loyal Christian Scientists whose teachers are deceased, absent, or disloyal, or those whose teachers, for insufficient cause, refuse to endorse their applications for membership with The Mother Church,—can apply to the Clerk of this Church, and present to him a recommendation signed by three members thereof in good standing, after which, the unanimous vote of the Board of Directors may admit said applicant to membership.

Addressed to Clerk. SECTION 5. All applications for membership must be addressed to the Clerk of the Church.

Endorsing Applications. SECTION 6. A member of The Mother Church shall not endorse nor countersign an application for membership therewith until after the blank has been properly filled out by an applicant. A member who violates this By-Law shall be disciplined.

Notice of Rejection. SECTION 7. If an application for membership with The First Church of Christ, Scientist, in Boston, Mass., is rejected, the Clerk of the Church shall send to the applicant a notice of such rejection; but neither the Clerk nor the Church shall be obliged to report the cause for rejection.

Article VI—RECOMMENDATION AND ELECTION

Pupils of Normal Students. SECTION 1. One Normal student cannot recommend the pupil of another Normal student, so long as both are loyal to their Leader and to the Christian Science textbook, except as provided for in Article V, Sect. 4.

Members of The Mother Church. SECTION 2. Only members of The Mother Church are qualified to approve for membership individuals who are known to them to be Christians, and faithful, loyal students of the textbook, SCIENCE AND HEALTH WITH KEY TO THE SCRIPTURES. If the approver is not a loyal student of Mrs. Eddy, a Director of this Church, or a student of the Board of Education who holds a degree, the application must be countersigned by one of these.

Election. SECTION 3. Applicants for membership in this Church, whose applications are correctly prepared, may be elected by majority vote of the Christian Science Board of Directors at the semi-annual meetings held for this purpose.

Article VII—PROBATIONARY MEMBERSHIP

Members who once Withdrew. SECTION 1. Individuals who have heretofore been members of this Church, or were members of the Church of Christ, Scientist, organized in 1879 by Mary Baker Eddy, but who have voluntarily withdrawn, may be received into this Church on one year's probation, provided they are willing and anxious to live according to its requirements and make application for membership according to its By-Laws. If, at the expiration of said one year, they are found worthy, they shall be received into full membership, but if not found worthy their applications shall be void.

Members once Dismissed. SECTION 2. A full member or a probationary member, who has been excommunicated once, and who afterward, when sufficient time has elapsed thoroughly to test his sincerity, gives due evidence of having genuinely repented and of being radically reformed, shall be eligible to probationary membership upon a unanimous vote of the Christian Science Board of Directors.

Ineligible for Probation. SECTION 3. If a member has been twice notified of his excommunication, he shall not again be received into this Church.

DISCIPLINE

Article VIII—GUIDANCE OF MEMBERS

A Rule for Motives and Acts. SECTION 1. Neither
animosity nor mere personal attachment should impel the
motives or acts of the members of The Mother Church. In
Science, divine Love alone governs man; and a Christian
Scientist reflects the sweet amenities of Love, in rebuking
sin, in true brotherliness, charitableness, and forgiveness.
The members of this Church should daily watch and pray to
be delivered from all evil, from prophesying, judging,
condemning, counseling, influencing or being influenced
erroneously.

To be Read in Church. SECTION 2. The above Church
Rule shall be read in The Mother Church and in the branch
churches by the First Reader on the first Sunday of each
month. On Communion day the Church Tenets are to be
read.

Christ Jesus the Ensample. SECTION 3. He who dated the
Christian era is the Ensample in Christian Science. Careless
comparison or irreverent reference to Christ Jesus is
abnormal in a Christian Scientist, and is prohibited. When
it is necessary to show the great gulf between Christian
Science and theosophy, hypnotism, or spiritualism, do it,
but without hard words. The wise man saith, "A soft
answer turneth away wrath." However despitefully used
and misrepresented by the churches or the press, in return
employ no violent invective, and do good unto your
enemies when the opportunity occurs. A departure from
this rule disqualifies a member for office in the Church or
on the Board of Lectureship, and renders this member

liable to discipline and, possibly, dismissal from The Mother Church.

Daily Prayer. SECTION 4. It shall be the duty of every member of this Church to pray each day: "Thy kingdom come;" let the reign of divine Truth, Life, and Love be established in me, and rule out of me all sin; and may Thy Word enrich the affections of all mankind, and govern them!

Prayer in Church. SECTION 5. The prayers in Christian Science churches shall be offered for the congregations collectively and exclusively.

Alertness to Duty. SECTION 6. It shall be the duty of every member of this Church to defend himself daily against aggressive mental suggestion, and not be made to forget nor to neglect his duty to God, to his Leader, and to mankind. By his works he shall be judged,—and justified or condemned.

One Christ. SECTION 7. In accordance with the Christian Science textbooks,—the BIBLE, and SCIENCE AND HEALTH WITH KEY TO THE SCRIPTURES,—and in accord with all of Mrs. Eddy's teachings, members of this Church shall neither entertain a belief nor signify a belief in more than one Christ, even that Christ whereof the Scripture beareth testimony.

No Malpractice. SECTION 8. Members will not intentionally or knowingly mentally malpractise, inasmuch as Christian Science can only be practised according to the Golden Rule: "All things whatsoever ye would that men should do to you, do ye even so to them." (Matt. 7:12.)

A member of The Mother Church who mentally malpractises upon or treats our Leader or her staff without her or their consent shall be disciplined, and a second offense as aforesaid shall cause the name of said member to be dropped forever from The Mother Church.

Formulas Forbidden. SECTION 9. No member shall use written formulas, nor permit his patients or pupils to use them, as auxiliaries to teaching Christian Science or for healing the sick. Whatever is requisite for either is contained in the books of the Discoverer and Founder of Christian Science. Sometimes she may strengthen the faith by a written text as no one else can.

No Adulterating Christian Science. SECTION 10. A member of this Church shall not publish profuse quotations from Mary Baker Eddy's copyrighted works without her permission, and shall not plagiarize her writings. This By-Law not only calls more serious attention to the commandment of the Decalogue, but tends to prevent Christian Science from being adulterated.

No Incorrect Literature. SECTION 11. A member of this Church shall neither buy, sell, nor circulate Christian Science literature which is not correct in its statement of the divine Principle and rules and the demonstration of Christian Science. Also the spirit in which the writer has written his literature shall be definitely considered. His writings must show strict adherence to the Golden Rule, or his literature shall not be adjudged Christian Science. A departure from the spirit or letter of this By-Law involves schisms in our Church and the possible loss, for a time, of Christian Science.

Obnoxious Books. SECTION 12. A member of this Church shall not patronize a publishing house or bookstore that has for sale obnoxious books.

Per Capita Tax. SECTION 13. Every member of The Mother Church shall pay annually a per capita tax of not less than one dollar, which shall be forwarded each year to the Church Treasurer.

Church Periodicals. SECTION 14. It shall be the privilege and duty of every member, who can afford it, to subscribe for the periodicals which are the organs of this Church; and it shall be the duty of the Directors to see that these periodicals are ably edited and kept abreast of the times.

Church Organizations Ample. SECTION 15. Members of this Church shall not unite with organizations which impede their progress in Christian Science. God requires our whole heart, and he supplies within the wide channels of The Mother Church dutiful and sufficient occupation for all its members.

Joining Another Society. SECTION 16. It shall be the duty of the members of The Mother Church and of its branches to promote peace on earth and good will toward men; but members of The Mother Church shall not hereafter become members of other societies except those specified in the Mother Church Manual, and they shall strive to promote the welfare of all mankind by demonstrating the rules of divine Love.

Forbidden Membership. SECTION 17. A member of The First Church of Christ, Scientist, in Boston, Mass., shall not be a member of any church whose Readers are not Christian Scientists and members of The Mother Church.

Officious Members. SECTION 18. A member of The Mother Church is not entitled to hold office or read in branch churches of this denomination except by invitation.

Legal Titles. SECTION 19. Students of Christian Science must drop the titles of Reverend and Doctor, except those who have received these titles under the laws of the State.

Illegal Adoption. SECTION 20. No person shall be a member of this Church who claims a spiritually adopted child or a spiritually adopted husband or wife. There must be legal adoption and legal marriage, which can be verified according to the laws of our land.

Use of Initials "C.S." SECTION 21. A member of The Mother Church shall not place the initials "C.S." after his name on circulars, cards, or leaflets, which advertise his business or profession, except as a Christian Science practitioner.

Practitioners and Patients. SECTION 22. Members of this Church shall hold in sacred confidence all private communications made to them by their patients; also such information as may come to them by reason of their relation of practitioner to patient. A failure to do this shall subject the offender to Church discipline.

A member of The Mother Church shall not, under pardonable circumstances, sue his patient for recovery of payment for said member's practice, on penalty of discipline and liability to have his name removed from membership. Also he shall reasonably reduce his price in chronic cases of recovery, and in cases where he has not effected a cure. A Christian Scientist is a humanitarian; he is benevolent, forgiving, long-suffering, and seeks to overcome evil with good.

Duty to Patients. SECTION 23. If a member of this Church has a patient whom he does not heal, and whose case he cannot fully diagnose, he may consult with an M. D. on the anatomy involved. And it shall be the privilege of a Christian Scientist to confer with an M. D. on Ontology, or the Science of being.

Testimonials. SECTION 24. "Glorify God in your body, and in your spirit, which are God's" (St. Paul). Testimony in regard to the healing of the sick is highly important. More than a mere rehearsal of blessings, it scales the pinnacle of praise and illustrates the demonstration of Christ, "who healeth all thy diseases" (Psalm 103:3). This testimony, however, shall not include a description of symptoms or of suffering, though the generic name of the disease may be indicated. This By-Law applies to testimonials which appear in the periodicals and to those which are given at the Wednesday evening meeting.

Charity to All. SECTION 25. While members of this Church do not believe in the doctrines of theosophy, hypnotism, or spiritualism, they cherish no enmity toward those who do believe in such doctrines, and will not harm them. But whenever God calls a member to bear testimony to Truth and to defend the Cause of Christ, he shall do it with love and without fear.

Uncharitable Publications. SECTION 26. A member of this Church shall not publish, nor cause to be published, an article that is uncharitable or impertinent towards religion, medicine, the courts, or the laws of our land.

The Golden Rule. SECTION 27. A member of The Mother Church shall not haunt Mrs. Eddy's drive when she goes out, continually stroll by her house, or make a summer resort near her for such a purpose.

Numbering the People. SECTION 28. Christian Scientists shall not report for publication the number of the members of The Mother Church, nor that of the branch churches. According to the Scripture they shall turn away from personality and numbering the people.

Our Church Edifices. SECTION 29. The periodicals of our denomination do not publish descriptions of our church edifices, but they may quote from other periodicals or give incidental narratives.

No Monopoly. SECTION 30. A Scientist shall not endeavor to monopolize the healing work in any church or locality, to the exclusion of others, but all who understand the teachings of Christian Science are privileged to enter into this holy work, and "by their fruits ye shall know them."

Christian Science Nurse. SECTION 31. A member of The Mother Church who represents himself or herself as a Christian Science nurse shall be one who has a demonstrable knowledge of Christian Science practice, who thoroughly understands the practical wisdom necessary in a sick room, and who can take proper care of the sick.

The cards of such persons may be inserted in The Christian Science Journal under rules established by the publishers.

Article IX—MARRIAGE AND DECEASE

A Legal Ceremony. SECTION 1. If a Christian Scientist is to be married, the ceremony shall be performed by a clergyman who is legally authorized.

Sudden Decease. SECTION 2. If a member of The Mother Church shall decease suddenly, without previous injury or illness, and the cause thereof be unknown, an autopsy shall be made by qualified experts. When it is possible the body of a female shall be prepared for burial by one of her own sex.

Article X—DEBATING IN PUBLIC

No Unauthorized Debating. SECTION 1. A member of this Church shall not debate on Christian Science in public debating assemblies, without the consent of the Board of Directors.

Article XI—COMPLAINTS

Departure from Tenets. SECTION 1. If a member of this Church shall depart from the Tenets and be found having the name without the life of a Christian Scientist, and another member in good standing shall from Christian motives make this evident, a meeting of the Board of Directors shall be called, and the offender's case shall be tried and said member exonerated, put on probation, or excommunicated.

Violation of By-Laws. SECTION 2. A member who is found violating any of the By-Laws or Rules herein set forth, shall be admonished in consonance with the Scriptural demand in Matthew 18:15-17; and if he neglect to accept such admonition, he shall be placed on probation, or if he repeat the offense, his name shall be dropped from the roll of Church membership.

Violation of Christian Fellowship. SECTION 3. Any member who shall unjustly aggrieve or vilify the Pastor Emeritus or another member, or who does not live in Christian fellowship with members who are in good and regular standing with this Church, shall either withdraw from the Church or be excommunicated.

Preliminary Requirement. SECTION 4. No church discipline shall ensue until the requirements according to the Scriptures, in Matthew 18:15-17, have been strictly obeyed, unless a By-Law governing the case provides for immediate action.

Authority. SECTION 5. The Christian Science Board of Directors has power to discipline, place on probation, remove from membership, or to excommunicate members of The Mother Church. Only the members of this Board shall be present at meetings for the examination of complaints against church members; and they alone shall vote on cases involving The Mother Church discipline.

Members in Mother Church Only. SECTION 6. A complaint against a member of The Mother Church, if said member belongs to no branch church and if this complaint is not for mental malpractice, shall be laid before this Board, and within ten days thereafter, the Clerk of the Church shall address a letter of inquiry to the member complained of as to the validity of the charge. If a member is found guilty of that whereof he is accused and his previous character has been good, his confession of his error and evidence of his compliance with our Church Rules shall be deemed sufficient by the Board for forgiveness for once, and the Clerk of the Church shall immediately so inform him. But a second offense shall dismiss a member from the Church.

Working Against the Cause. SECTION 7. If a member of this Church shall, mentally or otherwise, persist in working against the interests of another member, or the interests of our Pastor Emeritus and the accomplishment of what she understands is advantageous to this Church and to the Cause of Christian Science, or shall influence others thus to act, upon her complaint or the complaint of a member for her or for himself, it shall be the duty of the Board of Directors immediately to call a meeting, and drop forever the name of the member guilty of this offense from the roll of Church membership.

No Unchristian Conduct. SECTION 8. If a member of this Church were to treat the author of our textbook disrespectfully and cruelly, upon her complaint that member should be excommunicated. If a member, without her having requested the information, shall trouble her on subjects unnecessarily and without her consent, it shall be considered an offense.

Not to Learn Hypnotism. SECTION 9. Members of this Church shall not learn hypnotism on penalty of being excommunicated from this Church. No member shall enter a complaint of mental malpractice for a sinister purpose. If the author of SCIENCE AND HEALTH shall bear witness to the offense of mental malpractice, it shall be considered a sufficient evidence thereof.

Publications Unjust. SECTION 10. If a member of The
Mother Church publishes, or causes to be published, an
article that is false or unjust, hence injurious, to Christian
Science or to its Leader, and if, upon complaint by another
member, the Board of Directors finds that the offense has
been committed, the offender shall be suspended for not
less than three years from his or her office in this Church
and from Church membership.

The Mother Church of Christ, Scientist, Tenets. SECTION
11. If a member of The Mother Church of Christ, Scientist,
or a member of a branch of this Church break the rules of
its Tenets as to unjust and unmerciful conduct—on
complaint of Mrs. Eddy our Pastor Emeritus—and this
complaint being found valid, his or her name shall be
erased from The Mother Church and the branch church's
list of membership and the offender shall not be received
into The Mother Church or a branch church for twelve
years.

Special Offense. SECTION 12. If a member of this Church,
either by word or work, represents falsely to or of the
Leader and Pastor Emeritus, said member shall
immediately be disciplined, and a second similar offense
shall remove his or her name from membership in The
Mother Church.

Members of Branch Churches. SECTION 13. A member of
both The Mother Church and a branch Church of Christ,
Scientist, or a Reader, shall not report nor send notices to
The Mother Church, or to the Pastor Emeritus, of errors of
the members of their local church; but they shall strive to
overcome these errors. Each church shall separately and
independently discipline its own members,—if this sad
necessity occurs.

Article XII—TEACHERS

Probation. SECTION 1. For sufficient reasons it may be
decided that a teacher has so strayed as not to be fit for the
work of a Reader in church or a teacher of Christian
Science. Although repentant and forgiven by the Church
and retaining his membership, this weak member shall not
be counted loyal till after three years of exemplary
character. Then the Board of Directors may decide if his
loyalty has been proved by uniform maintenance of the life
of a consistent, consecrated Christian Scientist.

Misteaching. SECTION 2. If a member of this Church is
found trying to practise or to teach Christian Science
contrary to the statement thereof in its textbook, SCIENCE
AND HEALTH WITH KEY TO THE SCRIPTURES, it
shall be the duty of the Board of Directors to admonish that
member according to Article XI, Sect. 4. Then, if said
member persists in this offense, his or her name shall be
dropped from the roll of this Church.

MEETINGS

Article XIII—REGULAR AND SPECIAL MEETINGS

Annual Meetings. SECTION 1. The regular meetings of
The Mother Church shall be held annually, on Monday
following the first Sunday in June. No other than its of
officers are required to be present. These assemblies shall
be for listening to the reports of Treasurer, Clerk, and
Committees, and general reports from the Field.

Meetings of Board of Directors. SECTION 2. The annual
meeting of the Christian Science Board of Directors, for
electing officers and other business, shall be held on
Monday preceding the annual meeting of the Church.
Regular meetings for electing candidates to membership
with The Mother Church, and for the transaction of such
other business as may properly come before these
meetings, shall be held on the Friday preceding the first
Sunday in June, and on the first Friday in November of
each year. Special meetings may be held at any time upon
the call of the Clerk.

Called only by the Clerk. SECTION 3. Before calling a
meeting of the members of this Church (excepting its
regular sessions) it shall be the duty of the Clerk to inform
the Board of Directors and the Pastor Emeritus of his
intention, and to state definitely the purpose for which the
members are to convene. The Clerk must have the consent
of this Board and the Pastor Emeritus, before he can call
said meeting.

CHURCH SERVICES

Article XIV—THE CHRISTIAN SCIENCE PASTOR

Ordination. SECTION 1. I, Mary Baker Eddy, ordain the BIBLE, and SCIENCE AND HEALTH WITH KEY TO THE SCRIPTURES, Pastor over The Mother Church,— The First Church of Christ, Scientist, in Boston, Mass.,— and they will continue to preach for this Church and the world.

The Lesson-Sermon. SECTION 2. The subject of the Lesson-Sermon in the morning service of The Mother Church, and of the branch Churches of Christ, Scientist, shall be repeated at the other services on Sunday.

The correlative Biblical texts in the Lesson-Sermon shall extend from Genesis to Revelation.

Article XV—READING IN PUBLIC

Announcing Author's Name. SECTION 1. To pour into the ears of listeners the sacred revelations of Christian Science indiscriminately, or without characterizing their origin and thus distinguishing them from the writings of authors who think at random on this subject, is to lose some weight in the scale of right thinking. Therefore it is the duty of every member of this Church, when publicly reading or quoting from the books or poems of our Pastor Emeritus, first to announce the name of the author. Members shall also instruct their pupils to adopt the aforenamed method for the benefit of our Cause.

Article XVI—WELCOMING STRANGERS

The Leader's Welcome. SECTION 1. Mrs. Eddy welcomes to her seats in the church, persons of all sects and denominations who come to listen to the Sunday sermon and are not otherwise provided with seats.

The Local Members' Welcome. SECTION 2. It shall be the duty and privilege of the local members of The Mother Church to give their seats, if necessary, to strangers who may come to attend the morning services.

Article XVII—SERVICES UNINTERRUPTED

Continued Throughout the Year. SECTION 1. The services of The Mother Church shall be continued twelve months each year. One meeting on Sunday during the months of July and August is sufficient. A Christian Scientist is not fatigued by prayer, by reading the Scriptures or the Christian Science textbook. Amusement or idleness is weariness. Truth and Love rest the weary and heavy laden.

Easter Observances. SECTION 2. In the United States there shall be no special observances, festivities, nor gifts at the Easter season by members of The Mother Church. Gratitude and love should abide in every heart each day of all the years. Those sacred words of our beloved Master, "Let the dead bury their dead," and "Follow thou me," appeal to daily Christian endeavors for the living whereby to exemplify our risen Lord.

Laying a Corner Stone. SECTION 3. No large gathering of people nor display shall be allowed when laying the Corner

Stone of a Church of Christ, Scientist. Let the ceremony be devout. No special trowel should be used. (See SCIENCE AND HEALTH, page 140.)

Overflow Meetings. SECTION 4. A Church of Christ, Scientist, shall not hold two or more Sunday services at the same hour.

Article XVIII—COMMUNION

No more Communion. SECTION 1. The Mother Church of Christ, Scientist, shall observe no more Communion seasons.

Communion of Branch Churches. SECTION 2. The Communion shall be observed in the branch churches on the second Sunday in January and July of each year, and at this service the Tenets of The Mother Church are to be read.

Article XIX—MUSIC IN THE CHURCH

Soloist and Organist. SECTION 1. The music in The Mother Church shall not be operatic, but of an appropriate religious character and of a recognized standard of musical excellence; it shall be played in a dignified and suitable manner. Music from the organ alone should continue about eight or nine minutes for the voluntary and six or seven minutes for the postlude, the offertory conforming to the time required to take the collection. The solo singer shall not neglect to sing any special hymn selected by the Board of Directors.

Article XX—SUNDAY SCHOOL

The Sunday School. SECTION 1. Pupils may be received in the Sunday School classes of any Church of Christ, Scientist, up to the age of twenty years, and by transfer from another Church of Christ, Scientist, up to that age, but no pupil shall remain in the Sunday School of any Church of Christ, Scientist, after reaching the age of twenty. None except the officers, teachers, and pupils should attend the Sunday School exercises.

Teaching the Children. SECTION 2. The Sabbath School children shall be taught the Scriptures, and they shall be instructed according to their understanding or ability to grasp the simpler meanings of the divine Principle that they are taught.

Subject for Lessons. SECTION 3. The first lessons of the children should be the Ten Commandments (Exodus 20: 3-17), the Lord's Prayer (Matt. 6: 9-13), and its Spiritual Interpretation by Mary Baker Eddy, Sermon on the Mount (Matt. 5: 3-12). The next lessons consist of such questions and answers as are adapted to a juvenile class, and may be found in the Christian Science Quarterly Lessons, read in Church services. The instruction given by the children's teachers must not deviate from the absolute Christian Science contained in their textbook.

READING ROOMS

Article XXI

Establishment. SECTION 1. Each church of the Christian Science denomination shall have a Reading Room, though two or more churches may unite in having Reading Rooms, provided these rooms are well located.

Librarian. SECTION 2. The individuals who take charge of the Reading Rooms of The Mother Church shall be elected by the Christian Science Board of Directors, subject to the approval of Mary Baker Eddy. He or she shall have no bad habits, shall have had experience in the Field, shall be well educated, and a devout Christian Scientist.[3]

Literature in Reading Rooms. SECTION 3. The literature sold or exhibited in the reading rooms of Christian Science Churches shall consist only of Science and Health with Key to the Scriptures, by Mary Baker Eddy, and other writings by this author; also the literature published or sold by The Christian Science Publishing Society.

[3] See also Article XXV, Sect. 7.

RELATION AND DUTIES OF MEMBERS TO PASTOR EMERITUS

Article XXII

The Title of Mother Changed. SECTION 1. In the year eighteen hundred and ninety-five, loyal Christian Scientists had given to the author of their textbook, the Founder of Christian Science, the individual, endearing term of Mother. At first Mrs. Eddy objected to being called thus, but afterward consented on the ground that this appellative in the Church meant nothing more than a tender term such as sister or brother. In the year nineteen hundred and three and after, owing to the public misunderstanding of this name, it is the duty of Christian Scientists to drop the word mother and to substitute Leader, already used in our periodicals.

A Member not a Leader. SECTION 2. A member of The First Church of Christ, Scientist, in Boston, Mass., shall not be called Leader by members of this Church, when this term is used in connection with Christian Science.

Obedience Required. SECTION 3. It shall be the duty of the officers of this Church, of the editors of the Christian Science Journal, Sentinel, and Der Herold, of the members of the Committees on Publication, of the Trustees of The Christian Science Publishing Society, and of the Board of Education promptly to comply with any written order, signed by Mary Baker Eddy, which applies to their official functions. Disobedience to this By-Law shall be sufficient cause for the removal of the offending member from office.

The vacancy shall be supplied by a majority vote of the Christian Science Board of Directors, and the candidate shall be subject to the approval of Mary Baker Eddy.

Understanding Communications. SECTION 4. If the Clerk of this Church shall receive a communication from the Pastor Emeritus which he does not fully understand, he shall inform her of this fact before presenting it to the Church and obtain a clear understanding of the matter,— then act in accordance therewith.

Interpreting Communications. SECTION 5. If at a meeting of this Church a doubt or disagreement shall arise among the members as to the signification of the communications of the Pastor Emeritus to them, before action is taken it shall be the duty of the Clerk to report to her the vexed question and to await her explanation thereof.

Reading and Attesting Letters. SECTION 6. When a letter or a message from the Pastor Emeritus is brought before a meeting of this Church, or she is referred to as authority for business, it shall be the duty of the Church to inquire if all of the letter has been read, and to require all of it to be read; also to have any authority supposed to come from her satisfactorily attested.

Unauthorized Reports. SECTION 7. Members of this Church shall not report on authority an order from Mrs. Eddy that she has not sent, either to the Boards or to the executive bodies of this Church. The Pastor Emeritus is not to be consulted on cases of discipline, on the cases of candidates for admission to this Church, or on the cases of those on trial for dismissal from the Church.

Private Communications. SECTION 8. A strictly private communication from the Pastor Emeritus to a member of her Church shall not be made public without her written consent.

Unauthorized Legal Action. SECTION 9. A member of this Church shall not employ an attorney, nor take legal action on a case not provided for in its By-Laws—if said case relates to the person or to the property of Mary Baker Eddy—without having personally conferred with her on said subject.

Duty to God. SECTION 10. Members of this Church who turn their attention from the divine Principle of being to personality, sending gifts, congratulatory despatches or letters to the Pastor Emeritus on Thanksgiving, Christmas, New Year, or Easter, break a rule of this Church and are amenable therefor.

Opportunity for Serving the Leader. SECTION 11. At the written request of the Pastor Emeritus, Mrs. Eddy, the Board of Directors shall immediately notify a person who has been a member of this Church at least three years to go in ten days to her, and it shall be the duty of the member thus notified to remain with Mrs. Eddy three years consecutively. A member who leaves her in less time without the Directors' consent or who declines to obey this call to duty, upon Mrs. Eddy's complaint thereof shall be excommunicated from The Mother Church. Members thus serving the Leader shall be paid semi-annually at the rate of one thousand dollars yearly in addition to rent and board. Those members whom she teaches the course in Divinity, and who remain with her three consecutive years, receive the degree of the Massachusetts Metaphysical College.

Location. SECTION 12. Rev. Mary Baker Eddy calls to her home or allows to visit or to locate therein only those individuals whom she engages through the Christian Science Board of Directors of the Mother Church. This By-Law takes effect on Dec. 15, 1908.

Agreement Required. SECTION 13. When the Christian Science Board of Directors calls a student in accordance with Article XXII, Sect. 11, of our Church Manual to the home of their Leader, Mrs. Eddy, said student shall come under a signed agreement to remain with Mrs. Eddy if she so desires, during the time specified in the Church Manual.

Incomplete Term of Service. SECTION 14. If a student who has been called to serve our Leader in accordance with Article XXII, Sect. 11, of the Church Manual leaves her before the expiration of the time therein mentioned such student shall pay to Mrs. Eddy whatsoever she may charge for what she has taught him or her during the time of such service.

Help. SECTION 15. If the author of the Christian Science textbook call on this Board for household help or a handmaid, the Board shall immediately appoint a proper member of this Church therefor, and the appointee shall go immediately in obedience to the call. "He that loveth father or mother more than me is not worthy of me." (Matt. 10:37.)

Students with Mrs. Eddy. SECTION 16. Students employed by Mrs. Eddy at her home shall not take care of their churches or attend to other affairs outside of her house.

Mrs. Eddy's Room. SECTION 17. The room in The Mother Church formerly known as "Mother's Room" shall hereafter be closed to visitors.

Pastor Emeritus to be Consulted. SECTION 18. The Mother Church shall not make a church By-Law, nor enter into a business transaction with a Christian Scientist in the employ of Rev. Mary Baker Eddy, without first consulting her on said subject and adhering strictly to her advice thereon.

THE MOTHER CHURCH AND BRANCH CHURCHES

Article XXIII

Local Self-government. SECTION 1. The Mother Church of Christ, Scientist, shall assume no general official control of other churches, and it shall be controlled by none other. Each Church of Christ, Scientist, shall have its own form of government. No conference of churches shall be held, unless it be when our churches, located in the same State, convene to confer on a statute of said State, or to confer harmoniously on individual unity and action of the churches in said State.

Titles. SECTION 2. "The First Church of Christ, Scientist," is the legal title of The Mother Church. Branch churches of The Mother Church may take the title of First Church of Christ, Scientist; Second Church of Christ, Scientist; and so on, where more than one church is established in the same place; but the article "The" must not be used before titles of branch churches, nor written on applications for membership in naming such churches.

Mother Church Unique. SECTION 3. In its relation to other Christian Science churches, in its By-Laws and self-government, The Mother Church stands alone; it occupies a position that no other church can fill. Then for a branch church to assume such position would be disastrous to Christian Science. Therefore, no Church of Christ, Scientist, shall be considered loyal that has branch churches or adopts The Mother Church's form of government, except in such cases as are specially allowed and named in this Manual.

41

Tenets Copyrighted. SECTION 4. Branch churches shall not write the Tenets of The Mother Church in their church books, except they give the name of their author and her permission to publish them as Tenets of The Mother Church, copyrighted in SCIENCE AND HEALTH WITH KEY TO THE SCRIPTURES.

Manual. SECTION 5. Branch churches shall not adopt, print, nor publish the Manual of The Mother Church. See Article XXXV, Sect. 1.

Organizing Churches. SECTION 6. A member of this Church who obeys its By-Laws and is a loyal exemplary Christian Scientist working in the Field, is eligible to form a church in conformity with Sect. 7 of this Article, and to have church services conducted by reading the SCRIPTURES and the Christian Science textbook. This church shall be acknowledged publicly as a Church of Christ, Scientist. Upon proper application, made in accordance with the rules of The Christian Science Publishing Society, the services of such a church may be advertised in The Christian Science Journal. The branch churches shall be individual, and not more than two small churches shall consolidate under one church government. If the Pastor Emeritus, Mrs. Eddy, should relinquish her place as the head or Leader of The Mother Church of Christ, Scientist, each branch church shall continue its present form of government in consonance with The Mother Church Manual.

Requirements for Organizing Branch Churches. SECTION 7. A branch church of The First Church of Christ, Scientist, Boston, Mass., shall not be organized with less than sixteen loyal Christian Scientists, four of whom are members of The Mother Church. This membership shall include at least one active practitioner whose card is published in the list of practitioners in The Christian Science Journal.

Privilege of Members. SECTION 8. Members in good standing with The Mother Church, who are members of the faculty, instructors, or students organization.

No Close Communion. SECTION 9. The Mother Church and the branch churches shall not confine their membership to the pupils of one teacher.

No Interference. SECTION 10. A member of The Mother Church may be a member of one branch Church of Christ, Scientist, or of one Christian Science society holding public services, but he shall not be a member of both a branch church and a society; neither shall he exercise supervision or control over any other church. In Christian Science each branch church shall be distinctly democratic in its government, and no individual, and no other church shall interfere with its affairs.

Teachers' and Practitioners' Offices. SECTION 11. Teachers and practitioners of Christian Science shall not have their offices or rooms in the branch churches, in the reading rooms, nor in rooms connected therewith.

Recognition. SECTION 12. In order to be eligible to a card in The Christian Science Journal, churches and societies are required to acknowledge as such all other Christian Science churches and societies advertised in said Journal, and to maintain toward them an attitude of Christian fellowship.

GUARDIANSHIP OF CHURCH FUNDS

Article XXIV

Church Edifice a Testimonial. SECTION 1. Whereas, on March 20, 1895, the Christian Science Board of Directors, in behalf of The First Church of Christ, Scientist, Boston, Mass., presented to Rev. Mary Baker Eddy their church edifice as a Testimonial of this Church's love and gratitude, and she, with grateful acknowledgments thereof, declined to receive this munificent gift, she now understands the financial situation between the Christian Science Board of Directors and said Church to be as follows:—

Financial Situation. SECTION 2. The Christian Science Board of Directors owns the church edifices, with the land whereon they stand, legally; and the Church members own the aforesaid premises and buildings, beneficially. After the first church was built, the balance of the building funds, which remained in the hands of the Directors, belonged to the Church, and not solely to the Directors. The balance of the church building funds, which can be spared after the debts are paid, should remain on safe deposit, to be hereafter used for the benefit of this Church, as the right occasion may call for it. The following indicates the proper management of the Church funds:—

Report of Directors. SECTION 3. It shall be the duty of the Christian Science Board of Directors to have the books of the Church Treasurer audited semi-annually, and to report at the annual Church meeting the amount of funds which the Church has on hand, the amount of its indebtedness and of its expenditures for the last year.

Finance Committee. SECTION 4. There shall be a Committee on Finance, which shall consist of three members of this Church in good standing. Its members shall be appointed annually by the Christian Science Board of Directors and with the consent of the Pastor Emeritus. They shall hold quarterly meetings and keep themselves thoroughly informed as to the real estate owned by this Church and the amount of funds received by the Treasurer of The Mother Church, who is individually responsible for said funds. They shall have the books of the Christian Science Board of Directors and the books of the Church Treasurer audited annually by an honest, competent accountant. The books are to be audited on May first.

Prior to paying bills against the Church, the Treasurer of this Church shall submit them all to said committee for examination.

This committee shall decide thereupon by a unanimous vote, and its endorsement of the bills shall render them payable.

If it be found that the Church funds have not been properly managed, it shall be the duty of the Board of Directors and the Treasurer to be individually responsible for the performance of their several offices satisfactorily, and for the proper distribution of the funds of which they are the custodians.

God's Requirement. SECTION 5. God requires wisdom, economy, and brotherly love to characterize all the proceedings of the members of The Mother Church, The First Church of Christ, Scientist.

Provision for the Future. SECTION 6. In case of any possible future deviation from duty, the Committee on Finance shall visit the Board of Directors, and, in a Christian spirit and manner, demand that each member thereof comply with the By-Laws of the Church. If any Director fails to heed this admonition, he may be dismissed from office and the vacancy supplied by the Board.

Debt and Duty. SECTION 7. The Mother Church shall not be made legally responsible for the debts of individuals except such debts as are specified in its By-Laws. Donations from this Church shall not be made without the written consent of the Pastor Emeritus. Also important movements of the manager of the Committee on Publication shall be sanctioned by the Board of Directors and be subject to the approval of Mary Baker Eddy. (See Article I, Sect. 6.)

Emergencies. SECTION 8. The Treasurer, personally, or through the Clerk of the Church, may pay from the funds of the Church bills of immediate necessity not exceeding $200 for any one transaction, and he may keep on deposit the sum of $500 with the Clerk, as a petty cash fund, to be used by him for the payment of such bills. Such payments shall be reported, on the first of the following month, to the Board of Directors and the Committee on Finance, for their approval.

Committee on Business. SECTION 9. The Christian Science Board of Directors shall elect annually a Committee on Business, which shall consist of not less than three loyal members of The Mother Church, who shall transact promptly and efficiently such business as Mrs. Eddy, the Directors, or the Committee on Publication shall commit to it. While the members of this Committee are engaged in the transaction of the business assigned to them they shall be paid from the Church funds. Before being eligible for office the names of the persons nominated for said office shall be presented to Mrs. Eddy for her written approval.

THE CHRISTIAN SCIENCE PUBLISHING SOCIETY

Article XXV

Board of Trustees. SECTION 1. The Board of Trustees, constituted by a Deed of Trust given by Rev. Mary Baker Eddy, the Pastor Emeritus of this Church, on January twenty-fifth, 1898, shall hold and manage the property therein conveyed, and conduct the business of "The Christian Science Publishing Society" on a strictly Christian basis, for the promotion of the interests of Christian Science.

Disposal of Funds. SECTION 2. The net profits of the business shall be paid over semi-annually to the Treasurer of The Mother Church. He shall hold this money subject to the order of the Christian Science Board of Directors, which is authorized to order its disposition only in accordance with the By-Laws contained in this Manual.

Vacancies in Trusteeship. SECTION 3. The Christian Science Board of Directors shall have the power to declare vacancies in said trusteeship, for such reasons as to the Board may seem expedient.

Whenever a vacancy shall occur, the Pastor Emeritus reserves the right to fill the same by appointment; but if she does not elect to exercise this right, the remaining trustees shall fill the vacancy, subject to her approval.

Editors and Manager. SECTION 4. The term of office for the editors and the manager of The Christian Science Publishing Society is one year each, dating from the time of election to the office. Incumbents who have served one year or more can be re-elected, or new officers elected, by a unanimous vote of the Christian Science Board of Directors, and the consent of the Pastor Emeritus given in her own handwriting.

Suitable Employees. SECTION 5. A person who is not accepted by the Pastor Emeritus and the Christian Science Board of Directors as suitable, shall in no manner be connected with publishing her books, nor with editing or publishing The Christian Science Journal, Christian Science Sentinel, Der Herold der Christian Science, nor with The Christian Science Publishing Society.

Periodicals. SECTION 6. Periodicals which shall at any time be published by The Christian Science Publishing Society, shall be copyrighted and conducted according to the provisions in the Deed of Trust relating to The Christian Science Journal.

Rule of Conduct. SECTION 7. No objectionable pictures shall be exhibited in the rooms where the Christian Science textbook is published or sold. No idle gossip, no slander, no mischief-making, no evil speaking shall be allowed.

Books to be Published. SECTION 8. Only the Publishing Society of The Mother Church selects, approves, and publishes the books and literature it sends forth. If Mary Baker Eddy disapproves of certain books or literature, the Society will not publish them. The Committees on Publication are in no manner connected with these functions. A book or an article of which Mrs. Eddy is the author shall not be published nor republished by this Society without her knowledge or written consent.

Removal of Cards. SECTION 9. No cards shall be removed from our periodicals without the request of the advertiser, except by a majority vote of the Christian Science Board of Directors at a meeting held for this purpose or for the examination of complaints.

Members of this Church who practise other professions or pursue other vocations, shall not advertise as healers, excepting those members who are officially engaged in the work of Christian Science, and they must devote ample time for faithful practice.

TEACHING CHRISTIAN SCIENCE

Article XXVI—TEACHERS

Motive in Teaching. SECTION 1. Teaching Christian Science shall not be a question of money, but of morals and religion, healing and uplifting the race.

Care of Pupils. SECTION 2. Christian Scientists who are teachers shall carefully select for pupils such only as have good past records and promising proclivities toward Christian Science. A teacher shall not assume personal control of, or attempt to dominate his pupils, but he shall hold himself morally obligated to promote their progress in the understanding of divine Principle, not only during the class term but after it, and to watch well that they prove sound in sentiment and practical in Christian Science. He shall persistently and patiently counsel his pupils in conformity with the unerring laws of God, and shall enjoin them habitually to study the Scriptures and SCIENCE AND HEALTH WITH KEY TO THE SCRIPTURES as a help thereto.

Defense against Malpractice. SECTION 3. Teachers shall instruct their pupils how to defend themselves against mental malpractice, never to return evil for evil, but to know the truth that makes free, and thus to be a law, not unto others, but to themselves.

Number of Pupils. SECTION 4. The teachers of Christian Science shall teach but one class yearly, which class shall consist of not more than thirty pupils. After 1907, the

Board of Education shall have one class triennially, a Normal class not exceeding thirty pupils.

Pupil's Tuition. SECTION 5. A student's price for teaching Christian Science shall not exceed $100.00 per pupil.

Associations. SECTION 6. The associations of the pupils of loyal teachers shall convene annually. The pupils shall be guided by the BIBLE, and SCIENCE AND HEALTH, not by their teachers' personal views. Teachers shall not call their pupils together, or assemble a selected number of them, for more frequent meetings.

A Single Field of Labor. SECTION 7. A loyal teacher of Christian Science shall not teach another loyal teacher's pupil, except it be in the Board of Education. Outside of this Board each student occupies only his own field of labor. Pupils may visit each other's churches, and by invitation attend each other's associations.

Caring for Pupils of Strayed Members. SECTION 8. A loyal teacher of Christian Science may teach and receive into his association the pupils of another member of this Church who has so strayed as justly to be deemed, under the provisions of Article XII, Sect. 1, not ready to lead his pupils.

Teachers must have Certificates. SECTION 9. A member of this Church shall not teach pupils Christian Science unless he has a certificate to show that he has been taught by Mrs. Eddy or has taken a Normal Course at the Massachusetts Metaphysical College or in the Board of Education.

Such members who have not been continuously active and loyal Christian Scientists since receiving instruction as above, shall not teach Christian Science without the approval of The Christian Science Board of Directors.

Article XXVII—PUPILS

Authorized to Teach. SECTION 1. After a student's pupil has been duly authorized to be a teacher of Christian Science, or has been under the personal instruction of Mrs. Eddy, he is no longer under the jurisdiction of his former teacher.

Without Teachers. SECTION 2. Those beloved brethren whose teacher has left them, can elect an experienced Christian Scientist, who is not in charge of an association of students and who is ready for this high calling, to conduct the meetings of their association.

Basis for Teaching. SECTION 3. The teachers of the Normal class shall teach from the chapter Recapitulation in SCIENCE AND HEALTH WITH KEY TO THE SCRIPTURES, and from the Christian Science Platform, beginning on page 330 of the revised editions since 1902, and they shall teach nothing contrary thereto. The teachers of the Primary class shall instruct their pupils from the said chapter on "Recapitulation" only.

Church Membership. SECTION 4. Neither the Pastor Emeritus nor a member of this Church shall teach Roman Catholics Christian Science, except it be with the written consent of the authority of their Church. Choice of patients is left to the wisdom of the practitioner, and Mrs. Eddy is not to be consulted on this subject.

Class Teaching. SECTION 5. Members of The Mother Church who are authorized by its By-Laws to teach Christian Science, shall not solicit, or cause or permit others to solicit, pupils for their classes. No member of this Church shall advise against class instruction.

Teachers of Christian Science must have the necessary moral and spiritual qualifications to elucidate the Principle and rule of Christian Science, through the higher meaning of the Scriptures. "The less the teacher personally controls other minds, and the more he trusts them to the divine Truth and Love, the better it will be for both teacher and student." (Retrospection and Introspection, page 84.)

BOARD OF EDUCATION

Article XXVIII—ORGANIZATION

Officers. SECTION 1. There shall be a Board of Education, under the auspices of Mary Baker Eddy, President of the Massachusetts Metaphysical College, consisting of three members, a president, vice-president, and teacher of Christian Science. Obstetrics will not be taught.

Election. SECTION 2. The vice-president shall be elected annually by the Christian Science Board of Directors. Beginning with 1907, the teacher shall be elected every third year by said Board, and the candidate shall be subject to the approval of the Pastor Emeritus.

President not to be Consulted. SECTION 3. The President is not to be consulted by students on the question of applying for admission to this Board nor on their course or conduct. The students can confer with their teachers on subjects essential to their progress.

Presidency of College. SECTION 4. Should the President resign over her own signature or vacate her office of President of the Massachusetts Metaphysical College, a meeting of the Christian Science Board of Directors shall immediately be called, and the vice-president of the Board of Education being found worthy, on receiving her approval shall be elected to fill the vacancy.

Article XXIX—APPLICANTS AND GRADUATES

Normal Teachers. SECTION 1. Loyal students who have been taught in a Primary class by Mrs. Eddy and have practised Christian Science healing acceptably three years, and who present such credentials as are required to verify this fact, are eligible to receive the degree of C.S.D.

Qualifications. SECTION 2. Loyal Christian Scientists' pupils who so desire may apply to the Board of Education for instruction; and if they have practised Christian Science healing successfully three years and will furnish evidence of their eligibility therefor, they are eligible to enter the Normal class. All members of this class must be thorough English scholars.

Certificates. SECTION 3. Students are examined and given certificates by this Board if found qualified to receive them.

Article XXX—ACTION OF THE BOARD

Sessions. SECTION 1. The term of the Massachusetts Metaphysical College will open with the Board of Education on the first Wednesday of December. The sessions will continue not over one week. None but the teacher and members of the College class shall be present at the sessions, and no Primary classes shall be taught under the auspices of this Board.

Special Instruction. SECTION 2. Not less than two thorough lessons by a well qualified teacher shall be given to each Normal class on the subject of mental practice and malpractice. One student in the class shall prepare a paper on said subject that shall be read to the class, thoroughly discussed, and understood; this paper shall be given to the teacher, and he shall not allow it or a copy of it to remain, but shall destroy this paper.

Signatures. SECTION 3. The signature of the teacher and of the President of the College shall be on all certificates issued.

Remuneration and Free Scholarship. SECTION 4. Tuition of class instruction in the Board of Education shall be $100.00. The bearer of a card of free scholarship from the President, Rev. Mary Baker Eddy, shall be entitled to a free course in this department on presentation of the card to the teacher. Only the President gives free admission to classes.

Surplus Funds. SECTION 5. Any surplus funds left in the hands of the Board of Education shall be paid over annually to the Treasurer of The Mother Church.

Primary Students. SECTION 6. Students of Christian Science, duly instructed therein and with good moral records, not having the certificate of C.S.D. may enter the Normal class in the Board of Education, which will be held once in three years beginning A. D. 1907; provided their diplomas are for three consecutive years under Mrs. Eddy's daily conversation on Christian Science, or from the Massachusetts Meta-physical College Board of Education.

Healing Better than Teaching. SECTION 7. Healing the sick and the sinner with Truth demonstrates what we affirm of Christian Science, and nothing can substitute this demonstration. I recommend that each member of this Church shall strive to demonstrate by his or her practice, that Christian Science heals the sick quickly and wholly, thus proving this Science to be all that we claim for it.

If both husband and wife are found duly qualified to teach Christian Science, either one, not both, should teach yearly one class.

Not Members of The Mother Church. SECTION 8. No person shall receive instructions in Christian Science in any class in the Massachusetts Metaphysical College, nor receive the degree of C.S.B. or C.S.D., who is not a member of The First Church of Christ, Scientist, in Boston, Mass.

Only those persons who are members of this Church and possessed of the qualifications named in Sect. 9 of Article XXVI of these By-Laws shall be deemed loyal teachers of Christian Science.

BOARD OF LECTURESHIP

Article XXXI—ORGANIZATION AND DUTIES

Election. SECTION 1. This Church shall maintain a Board of Lectureship, the members of which shall be elected annually on Monday preceding the Annual Meeting, subject to the approval of the Pastor Emeritus. The lecture year shall begin July 1 of each year.

Duty of Lecturers. SECTION 2. It is the duty of the Board of Lectureship to include in each lecture a true and just reply to public topics condemning Christian Science, and to bear testimony to the facts pertaining to the life of the Pastor Emeritus. Each member shall mail to the Clerk of this Church copies of his lectures before delivering them.

No Disruption of Branch Churches. SECTION 3. The Board of Lectureship is not allowed in anywise to meddle with nor to disrupt the organization of branch churches. The lecturer can invite churches within the city whither he is called to unite in their attendance on his lecture, and so make for their churches a less lecture fee; but the churches shall decide their action.

Receptions. SECTION 4. As a rule there should be no receptions nor festivities after a lecture on Christian Science, but there may occur exceptions. If there be an individual who goes to hear and deride truth, he should go away contemplating truth; and he who goes to seek truth should have the opportunity to depart in quiet thought on that subject.

Circuit Lecturer. SECTION 5. Upon the written request of Mrs. Eddy, The Mother Church shall appoint a Circuit Lecturer. His term of office, if approved, shall not be less than three years. He shall lecture in the United States, in Canada, in Great Britain and Ireland.

A member shall neither resign nor transfer this sacred office.

Article XXXII—CALLS FOR LECTURES

The Directors. SECTION 1. When the need is apparent, the Christian Science Board of Directors of The Mother Church may call on any member of this Board of Lectureship to lecture at such places and at such times as the cause of Christian Science demands.

From Branch Churches. SECTION 2. The branch Churches of Christ, Scientist, may apply through their clerks to a member of this Board of Lectureship for a speaker, and one shall be assigned them by the Board.

From Societies. SECTION 3. If called for, a member of the Board may lecture for a Society.

Annual Lectures. SECTION 4. The Mother Church and the branch churches shall call on the Board of Lectureship annually for one or more lectures.

No Lectures by Readers. SECTION 5. No lecture shall be given by a Reader during his term of Readership. The duties alone of a Reader are ample.

No Wednesday Evening Lectures. SECTION 6. The Board of Lectureship shall not appoint a lecture for Wednesday evening.

Lecture Fee. SECTION 7. The lecture fee shall be left to the discretion of the lecturer.

Expenses. SECTION 8. The lecturer's traveling expenses and the cost of hall shall be paid by the church that employs him.

Exceptional Cases. SECTION 9. If a lecturer receive a call to lecture in a place where he sees there is special need, and the local church is unable to meet the expense, he is at liberty to supply that need and trust to contributions for his fee.

COMMITTEE ON PUBLICATION

Article XXXIII

In The Mother Church. SECTION 1. There shall be
appointed by The Mother Church a Committee on
Publication, which shall consist of one loyal Christian
Scientist who lives in Boston, and he shall be manager of
the Committees on Publication throughout the United
States, Canada, Great Britain and Ireland. He shall be
elected annually by a unanimous vote of the Christian
Science Board of Directors and the consent of the Pastor
Emeritus given in her own handwriting, and shall receive
an annual salary, paid quarterly, of not less than four
thousand dollars.

Duties. SECTION 2. It shall be the duty of the Committee
on Publication to correct in a Christian manner impositions
on the public in regard to Christian Science, injustices done
Mrs. Eddy or members of this Church by the daily press, by
periodicals or circulated literature of any sort. This
Committee on Publication shall be responsible for
correcting or having corrected a false newspaper article
which has not been replied to by other Scientists, or which
has been forwarded to this Committee for the purpose of
having him reply to it. If the correction by the Committee
on Publication is not promptly published by the periodical
in which it is desirable that this correction shall appear, this
Committee shall immediately apply for aid to the
Committee on Business. Furthermore, the Committee on
Publication shall read the last proof sheet of such an article
and see that it is published according to copy; he shall
circulate in large quantities the papers containing such an

article, sending a copy to the Clerk of the Church. It shall also be the duty of the Committee on Publication to have published each year in a leading Boston newspaper the letter sent to the Pastor Emeritus by the Church members in annual meeting assembled. The State Committees on Publication act under the direction of this Committee on Publication.

In Branch Churches. SECTION 3. The Readers of the three largest branch churches in each State of the United States and in Canada shall annually and alternately appoint a Committee on Publication to serve in their localities. For the purposes of this By-Law, the State of California shall be considered as though it were two States, the dividing line being the 36th parallel of latitude. Each county of Great Britain and Ireland, except as hereinafter specified, through the Readers of its three largest branch churches, shall annually and alternately appoint a Committee on Publication to serve in its locality. Each church is not necessarily confined to its own members in selecting this Committee, but if preferred, can appoint a Committee on Publication who is in good fellowship with another Church of Christ, Scientist.

This By-Law applies to all States except Massachusetts, in which the Committee on Publication is elected only by the Christian Science Board of Directors. The Committee for the counties in which London, England, is situated shall be appointed by the Christian Science Board of Directors, and he shall, in addition to his other duties, act as District Manager of the Committees on Publication for Great Britain and Ireland.

Appointment. SECTION 4. The Committees on Publication shall consist of men generally. Each State Committee shall be appointed by the First and Second Readers of the church employing said Committee. If prior to the meeting of the church for the election of officers, Mrs. Eddy shall send to the First Reader of the church the name of a candidate for its Committee on Publication, the Readers shall appoint said candidate. Or if she shall send a special request to any Committee on Publication, the request shall be carried out according to her directions.

Removal from Office. SECTION 5. If the Committee on Publication neglects to fulfil the obligations of his office according to these By-Laws, and this becomes apparent to the Christian Science Board of Directors, it shall be the duty of the Directors immediately to act upon this important matter in accordance with said By-Laws.

The Christian Science Board of Directors may notify any Church of Christ, Scientist, to remove its Committee on Publication and to appoint another Committee to fill the vacancy; and it shall be the duty of that church to comply with this request. In such cases it shall be the privilege of this Board to name the Committee if it so desires, and any Committee so named by the Board shall be elected by the branch church.

Case of Necessity. SECTION 6. If a suitable man is not obtainable for Committee on Publication, a suitable woman shall be elected. If at any time the Christian Science Board of Directors shall determine that the manager of the general Committee on Publication needs an assistant, the Board shall, with the approval of the Pastor Emeritus, appoint an assistant manager, who shall receive an adequate salary from The Mother Church.

CHURCH-BUILDING

Article XXXIV

Building Committee. SECTION 1. There shall be a Building Committee consisting of not less than three members, and this committee shall not be dissolved until the new church edifice is completed. This committee shall elect, dismiss, or supply a vacancy of its members by a majority vote.

Designation of Deeds. SECTION 2. All deeds of further purchases of land for The First Church of Christ, Scientist, in Boston, Mass., shall have named in them all the trusts mentioned in the deeds given by Albert Metcalf and E. Noyes Whitcomb in March, 1903; but this rule shall not apply to land purchased for any purpose other than the erection of a church edifice. Also there shall be incorporated in all such deeds the phrase, "Mary Baker Eddy's Church, The Mother Church or The First Church of Christ, Scientist, in Boston, Mass."

The Mother Church Building. SECTION 3. The edifice erected in 1894 for The First Church of Christ, Scientist, in Boston, Mass., shall neither be demolished, nor removed from the site where it was built, without the written consent of the Pastor Emeritus, Mary Baker Eddy.

CHURCH MANUAL

Article XXXV

For The Mother Church Only. SECTION 1. The Church
Manual of The First Church of Christ, Scientist, in Boston,
Mass., written by Mary Baker Eddy and copyrighted, is
adapted to The Mother Church only. It stands alone,
uniquely adapted to form the budding thought and hedge it
about with divine Love. This Manual shall not be revised
without the written consent of its author.

Seventy-third Edition the Authority. SECTION 2. The
Board of Directors, the Committee on Bible Lessons, and
the Board of Trustees shall each keep a copy of the
Seventy-third Edition and of subsequent editions of the
Church Manual; and if a discrepancy appears in any revised
edition, these editions shall be cited as authority.

Amendment of By-Laws. SECTION 3. No new Tenet or
By-Law shall be adopted, nor any Tenet or By-Law
amended or annulled, without the written consent of Mary
Baker Eddy, the author of our textbook, SCIENCE AND
HEALTH.

Appendix

Special Instructions Regarding Applications for Church
Membership

1. Loyal members of The Mother Church are eligible to
approve candidates to unite with this Church.

2. No persons are eligible to countersign applications
except loyal students of Mrs. Eddy, Directors, and students
of the Board of Education who have been given a degree,
and are members of The Mother Church.

3. Those who approve applicants should have applications
returned to them after being filled out by the applicants, as
required by Article V, Sect. 6, and should compare them
with the forms here given, and see that names are legibly
written, before sending them to the Clerk of the Church. If
not correct, the applicant will be notified, and new
applications will be required, as none will be returned that
are not correctly made out. This requirement is to prevent
applications being duplicated and the confusion that might
result therefrom. It is important that these seemingly strict
conditions be exactly complied with, as the names of the
members of The Mother Church will be recorded in the
history of the Church and become a part thereof.

4. All names, whether of applicants, signers, or
countersigners, must be plainly written, and one, at least, of
the given names of each, written in full. Initials only of first
names will not be received. Women must sign Miss or Mrs.
before their names as the case may be.

All names must be written the same in all places where they are required.

TO APPLICANTS

1. In filling out the application blank, one of the Christian names must be written in full. Initials alone will not be received.

2. If the applicant is a married woman she must sign her own Christian name, not her husband's, and prefix her signature with "Mrs;" unmarried women must sign "Miss."

3. There are two regular forms of application. 1. For those who have studied Christian Science with an authorized teacher; 2. For those who have not studied Christian Science with a teacher.

Applicants will find the chief points of these instructions illustrated in Form 1 and Form 2, on pages 114 and 118.

4. Those whose teachers are deceased, absent, or disloyal, or those whose teachers refuse, without sufficient cause, to sign applications (see Art. V, Sect. 4), will be furnished special forms on application to the Clerk.

5. When branch churches are designated by number, as First Church, Second Church, etc., the number must be written First, Second, as shown on page 118. The article "the" either capitalized (The), or small (the), must not be used before titles of branch churches. See Article XXIII, Sect. 2.

6. If the applicant is not a member of a branch church, he should fill out his application in this respect according to the form on page 114.

APPLICATION FORMS

Application I

PROPERLY SIGNED AND ENDORSED,

ACCORDING TO ARTICLE V, SECT. 2

If you have been taught by a loyal student who has taken a degree at the Massachusetts Metaphysical College, or by one who has passed an examination by the Board of Education, fill this blank.

FORM 1

The First Church of Christ, Scientist, in Boston, Mass., is designed to be built on the rock of Christ—Truth and Life—and to reflect the Church Triumphant.

One who is not a member of any church, excepting a branch church of Christ, Scientist, who loves Christian Science, and reads understandingly the Bible, and SCIENCE AND HEALTH WITH KEY TO THE SCRIPTURES, by Reverend Mary Baker Eddy, and other works by this author, and who is Christianly qualified and can enter into full fellowship with the Tenets and Rules of

The First Church of Christ, Scientist, in Boston, Mass., is eligible to membership.

To The First Church of Christ, Scientist, in Boston, Mass.

Gordon V. Comer Clerk.

I hereby make application for membership, and subscribe to the

Tenets and the By-Laws of the Church.

My teacher in Christian Science is

...............James B. Brown, C.S.D. ....

I am not a member of any church.

FORM 1—(Continued)

I was formerly a member of the ....
.... denomination, but have definitely severed my connection therewith.

Name .... Mrs. Jennie W. Field, C.S. ....

Street and Number .... 18 Forest St., ...

Town or City .... Chicago, ...

State .... Ill ....

Date .... Jan. 2nd, 1901 ....

I cordially approve the applicant.

(a) .... James B. Brown, C.S.D. ....

Countersigned by ....

DO NOT DETACH.

To the applicant: Name ...... Mrs. Jennie W. Field, C.S.
...... Please fill out the Street and Number ... 18 Forest St.,
.... following for the use Town or City ....
Chicago, ... of the Treasurer of State
.... Ill ...... the Church:

Application I

PROPERLY SIGNED AND ENDORSED,

ACCORDING TO ARTICLE V, SECT. 2

If you have been taught by a loyal student who has taken a degree at the Massachusetts Metaphysical College, or by one who has passed an examination by the Board of Education, fill this blank.

FORM 1

The First Church of Christ, Scientist, in Boston, Mass., is designed to be built on the rock of Christ—Truth and Life—and to reflect the Church Triumphant.

One who is not a member of any church, excepting a branch church of Christ, Scientist, who loves Christian Science, and reads understandingly the Bible, and SCIENCE AND HEALTH WITH KEY TO THE SCRIPTURES, by Reverend Mary Baker Eddy, and other works by this author, and who is Christianly qualified and can enter into full fellowship with the Tenets and Rules of The First Church of Christ, Scientist, in Boston, Mass., is eligible to membership.

To The First Church of Christ, Scientist, in Boston, Mass.

Gordon V. Comer Clerk.

I hereby make application for membership, and subscribe to the

Tenets and the By-Laws of the Church.

My teacher in Christian Science is

.............James B. Brown, C.S.D. ....

I am not a member of any church, excepting Church of Christ,

Scientist, at ....

FORM 1—(Continued)

I was formerly a member of the ....
.... denomination, but have definitely severed my connection therewith.

Name .... Mrs. Jennie W. Field, C.S. ....

Street and Number ……. 18 Forest St., ……………

Town or City …………….. Chicago, ………………

State ……………………….. Ill ………………

Date …………….. Jan. 2nd, 1901 ………………

I cordially approve the applicant.

(a) ……………. James B. Brown, C.S.D. ……………

Countersigned by …………………………………

DO NOT DETACH.

To the applicant: Name …… Mrs. Jennie W. Field, C.S.
…… Please fill out the Street and Number … 18 Forest St.,
…….. following for the use Town or City …………
Chicago, ………. of the Treasurer of State
………………………. Ill …… the Church:

Application II

SIGNED, ENDORSED, AND COUNTERSIGNED,

ACCORDING TO ARTICLE VI, SECT. 2

If you have not been taught by a loyal student who has taken a degree at the Massachusetts Metaphysical College, or by one who has passed an examination by the Board of Education, fill this blank.

FORM 2

One who is not a member of any church, excepting a branch church of Christ, Scientist, who loves Christian Science, and reads understandingly the Bible, and SCIENCE AND HEALTH WITH KEY TO THE SCRIPTURES, by Reverend Mary Baker Eddy, and other works by this author, and who is Christianly qualified and can enter into full fellowship with the Tenets and Rules of The First Church of Christ, Scientist, in Boston, Mass., is eligible to membership.

To The First Church of Christ, Scientist, in Boston, Mass.

Gordon V. Comer Clerk.

I hereby make application for membership, and subscribe to the Tenets and the By-Laws of the Church. I have not studied Christian

Science with a teacher, and am not a member of any church excepting Second Church of Christ, Scientist, at New York, N.Y.

I was formerly a member of the ………………………..
…………. denomination, but have definitely severed my connection therewith.

FORM 2—(Continued)

Name ………….. Miss Emma L. French ……………..

Street and Number …… 293 Emerson St., ……………

Town or City ……………. New York ……………….

State ……………………….. N.Y. ……………..

Date …………….. Jan. 2nd, 1901 ……………….

I cordially approve the applicant.

(a) …………. Miss Mary E. Grant, C.S. ……………

Countersigned by .... James B. Brown, C.S.D. ....

DO NOT DETACH.

To the applicant: Name .... Miss Emma L. French ....
Please fill out the Street and Number .. 293 Emerson St. ...
following for the use Town or City .... New York
..... of the Treasurer of State .... N.Y. ...
the Church:

Present Order of Services in The Mother Church and
Branch Churches Republished from the Sentinel

SUNDAY SERVICES

1. Hymn.

2. Reading a Scriptural Selection.

3. Silent Prayer, followed by the audible repetition of the Lord's Prayer with its spiritual interpretation.

4. Hymn.

5. Announcing necessary notices.

6. Solo.

7. Reading the explanatory note on first leaf of Quarterly.

8. Announcing the subject of the Lesson Sermon, and reading the Golden Text.

9. Reading the Scriptural selection, entitled "Responsive Reading," alternately by the First Reader and the congregation.

10. Reading the Lesson-Sermon. (After the Second Reader reads the BIBLE references of the first Section of the Lesson, the First Reader makes the following announcement: "As announced in the explanatory note, I shall now read correlative passages from the Christian Science textbook, SCIENCE AND HEALTH WITH KEY TO THE SCRIPTURES, by Mary Baker Eddy.")

11. Collection.

12. Hymn.

13. Reading the scientific statement of being, and the correlative SCRIPTURE according to I John 3:1-3.

14. Pronouncing Benediction.

The services should be preceded and followed by organ or piano music of an appropriate character in all cases where this is possible.

On the first Sunday of each month Article VIII, SECT. 1, A Rule for Motives and Acts, is to be read.

WEDNESDAY MEETINGS

1. Hymn.

2. Reading from the BIBLE, and correlative passages from SCIENCE AND HEALTH WITH KEY TO THE SCRIPTURES.

3. Silent Prayer, followed by the audible repetition of the Lord's Prayer, its spiritual interpretation being omitted.

4. Hymn.

5. Announcing necessary notices.

6. Experiences, testimonies, and remarks on Christian Science.

7. Closing Hymn.

The services should be preceded and followed by organ or piano music of an appropriate character in all cases where this is possible.

Thanksgiving Day.

Order of Service for The Mother Church and Branch Churches.

1. Hymn.

2. Reading the Thanksgiving Proclamation of the President of the United States, or the Governor of the state, or both.

3. Reading a Scriptural Selection.

4. Silent Prayer, followed by the audible repetition of the Lord's Prayer with its spiritual interpretation.

5. Hymn.

6. Reading the Explanatory Note on the first leaf of the Quarterly.

7. Announcing the subject of the Lesson Sermon, and reading the Golden Text.

8. Responsive Reading by the First Reader and the congregation.

9. Reading the Lesson-Sermon prepared by the Bible Lesson Committee.

10. Solo.

11. Testimonies by Christian Scientists, appropriate for the occasion.

12. Hymn.

13. Reading the Scientific Statement of Being, and the correlative SCRIPTURE according to I John 3:1-3.

14. Pronouncing Benediction.

No collection is to be taken at this service.

The services should be preceded and followed by organ or piano music of an appropriate character in all cases where this is possible.

Present Order of Communion Services in Branch Churches

1. Hymn.

2. Reading a Scriptural Selection.

3. Silent Prayer, followed by the audible repetition of the Lord's Prayer with its spiritual interpretation.

4. Hymn.

5. Announcing necessary notices.

6. Reading Tenets of The Mother Church.

7. Collection and Solo.

8. Reading the explanatory note on first leaf of Quarterly.

9. Announcing the subject of the Lesson Sermon, and reading the Golden Text.

10. Reading the scriptural selection entitled "Responsive Reading" alternately by the First Reader and the congregation.

11. Reading the Lesson-Sermon. (After the Second Reader reads the BIBLE references of the first Section of the Lesson, the First Reader makes the following announcement: "As announced in the explanatory note, I

shall now read correlative passages from the Christian
Science textbook, SCIENCE AND HEALTH WITH KEY
TO THE SCRIPTURES, by Mary Baker Eddy.")

12. The First Reader briefly invites the congregation to
kneel in silent Communion. This is concluded by the
audible repetition of the Lord's Prayer (spiritual
interpretation omitted).

13. Singing the Doxology:

"Be Thou, O God, exalted high;

And as Thy glory fills the sky,

So let it be on earth displayed,

Till Thou art here and now obeyed."

14. Reading the scientific statement of being and the
correlative SCRIPTURE according to I John 3:1-3.

15. Pronouncing Benediction.

The Church Tenets shall be read at this service.

The services should be preceded and followed by organ or
piano music of an appropriate character in all cases where
this is possible.

Order of Exercises for the Sunday School of the Mother
Church.[4]

1. Call to order by the Superintendent.

2. Hymn.

3. Subject of the lesson announced; Golden Text repeated by the children; Responsive Reading.

4. Silent prayer, followed by the audible repetition of the Lord's Prayer in unison.

5. Instruction in classes, in accordance with Sections 2 and 3 of Article XX of the Manual of The Mother Church.

6. Entire school reassembles.

7. Hymn.

8. Scientific Statement of Being read by the Superintendent.

9. School dismissed.

[4] If a collection is taken, it should be taken in the classes before they reassemble.

Deed of Trust

The following is a Copy of the Deed of Trust Conveying Land for Church Edifice

KNOW ALL MEN BY THESE PRESENTS,

That I Mary Baker G. Eddy of Concord in the County of
Merrimack and State of New Hampshire in consideration
of one dollar to me paid by Ira O. Knapp of Boston,
Massachusetts, William B. Johnson of Boston,
Massachusetts, Joseph S. Eastaman of Chelsea,
Massachusetts, and Stephen A. Chase of Fall River,
Massachusetts, the receipt whereof is hereby
acknowledged, and, also in consideration of the trusts and
uses hereinafter mentioned and established, do hereby give,
bargain, sell, and convey to the said Ira O. Knapp, William
B. Johnson, Joseph S. Eastaman, and Stephen A. Chase as
trustees as hereinafter provided and to their legitimate
successors in office forever, a certain parcel of land situate
on Falmouth street in said Boston, bounded and described
as follows:

Beginning at the junction of Falmouth street, and a forty-
foot street now called Caledonia street; thence running
Southwest on said Falmouth street one hundred and sixteen
and eighty-eight hundredths feet; thence Northwest at a
right angle to a point where a line drawn at right angles to
said forty-foot street at a point thereon one hundred and
sixteen and fifty-five hundredths feet Northwest from the
point of beginning meets the said boundary at right angles
to Falmouth street, sixty-six and seventy-eight hundredths
feet; thence at an obtuse angle on said line at right angles to
said forty-foot street sixty-seven and thirty-five hundredths
feet to said forty-foot street; thence Southeasterly on said
forty-foot street one hundred and sixteen and fifty-five
hundredths feet to the point of beginning; containing seven
thousand eight hundred and twenty-eight square feet more
or less, and subject to the agreements and restrictions

mentioned in a deed recorded in Suffolk Registry of Deeds
Lib. 1719, Fol 83 so far as the same are now legally
operative.

This deed of conveyance is made upon the following
express trusts and conditions which the said grantees by
accepting this deed agree and covenant for themselves and
their successors in office to fully perform and fulfil.

1. Said grantees shall be known as the "Christian Science
Board of Directors," and shall constitute a perpetual body
or corporation under and in accordance with section one,
Chapter 39 of the Public Statutes of Massachusetts.[5]
Whenever a vacancy occurs in said Board the remaining
members shall within thirty days fill the same by election;
but no one shall be eligible to that office who is not in the
opinion of the remaining members of the Board a firm and
consistent believer in the doctrines of Christian Science as
taught in a book entitled "SCIENCE AND HEALTH," by
Mary Baker G. Eddy beginning with the seventy-first
edition thereof.

[5] The deacons, church wardens, or other similar officers
of Churches or religious societies, and the trustees of the
Methodist Episcopal churches, appointed according to the
discipline and usages thereof, shall, if citizens of this
commonwealth, be deemed bodies corporate for the
purpose of taking and holding in succession all grants and
donations, whether of real or personal estate, made either to
the and their successors, or to their respective churches, or
to the poor of their churches.

2. Said Board shall within five years from the date hereof
build or cause to be built upon said lot of land a suitable

and convenient church edifice, the cost of which shall not be less than fifty thousand dollars.

3. When said church building is completed said Board shall elect a pastor, reader or speaker to fill the pulpit who shall be a genuine Christian Scientist; they shall maintain public worship in accordance with the doctrines of Christian Science in said church, and for this purpose they are fully empowered to make any and all necessary rules and regulations.

4. Said Board of Directors shall not suffer or allow any building to be erected upon said lot except a church building or edifice, nor shall they allow said church building or any part thereof to be used for any other purpose than for the ordinary and usual uses of a church.

5. Said Board of Directors shall not allow or permit in said church building any preaching or other religious services which shall not be consonant and in strict harmony with the doctrines and practice of Christian Science as taught and explained by Mary Baker G. Eddy in the seventy-first edition of her book entitled "SCIENCE AND HEALTH," which is soon to be issued, and in any subsequent edition thereof.

6. The congregation which shall worship in said church shall be styled "The First Church of Christ, Scientist."

7. Said Directors shall not sell or mortgage the land hereby conveyed; but they shall see that all taxes and legal assessments on said property are promptly paid.

8. Said church building shall not be removed from said lot except for the purpose of rebuilding thereon a more

expensive or a more convenient structure in which said doctrines of Christian Science only shall be preached and practised. If said church building is removed for either of the purposes above set forth, any and all tablets and inscriptions which are or shall be upon said church building at the time of removal shall be removed therefrom and placed upon the walls of the new edifice. If said building is burned, the Directors shall forthwith proceed to rebuild the church.

9. Said Directors shall maintain regular preaching, reading or speaking in said church on each Sabbath, and an omission to have and maintain such preaching, reading or speaking for one year in succession shall be deemed a breach of this condition.

10. Whenever said Directors shall determine that it is inexpedient to maintain preaching, reading or speaking in said church in accordance with the terms of this deed, they are authorized and required to reconvey forthwith said lot of land with the building thereon to Mary Baker G. Eddy, her heirs and assigns forever by a proper deed of conveyance.

11. The omission or neglect on the part of said Directors to strictly comply with any of the conditions herein contained shall constitute a breach thereof, and the title hereby conveyed shall revert to the grantor Mary Baker G. Eddy, her heirs and assigns forever, upon her entry upon said land and taking possession thereof for such breach.

To Have and to Hold the above granted premises with all the privileges and appurtenances thereon belonging to said grantees and their successors in office to the uses and trusts above described forever.

And the said grantor for herself and her heirs, executors and administrators covenants with the said grantees and their successors in office that she is lawfully seized in fee simple of the aforesaid premises, that they are free from all incumbrances not herein mentioned or referred to, that she has good right to sell and convcy the same to the said grantees and their successors in office as aforesaid, and that she will and her heirs, executors, and administrators shall, warrant and defend the same to the said grantees and their successors in office forever against the lawful claims and demands of all persons.

In witness whereof I the said Mary Baker G. Eddy have hereto set my hand and seal this 1st day of September, 1892.

MARY BAKER G. EDDY.

Signed, sealed, and delivered in presence of

LAURA E. SARGENT.

R. E. WALKER.

September 1st, 1892.

STATE OF NEW HAMPSHIRE, MERRIMACK.

Then personally appeared the above named Mary Baker G. Eddy and acknowledged the foregoing instrument to be her free act and deed,

Before me

R. E. WALKER.

Notary Public.

September 2, 1892.

SUFFOLK REGISTRY OF DEEDS, Lib. 2081, Fol. 257.

Deed Conveying Land for Church Purposes

METCALE to KNAPP et al. Trs.

Libro 2886, Fol. 521.

KNOW ALL MEN,

That I, Albert Metcalf, the grantor in a certain deed given
to Ira O. Knapp and others dated October 23, 1896, and
recorded with Suffolk Deeds, Book 2591, page 398, do
hereby declare that the land conveyed by said deed was
conveyed to the grantees therein, as they are the Christian
Science Board of Directors, upon the trusts, but not subject
to the conditions mentioned in the deed creating said Board
given by Mary Baker G. Eddy to Ira O. Knapp and others,
dated September 1st, 1892, and recorded with Suffolk

Deeds, Book 2081, page 257. In addition to the trusts
contained in said deed of September 1, 1892, from Mary
Baker G. Eddy, this property is conveyed on the further
trusts that no new Tenet or By-Law shall be adopted, nor
any Tenet or By-Law amended or annulled by the grantees
unless the written consent of said Mary Baker G. Eddy, the
author of the textbook "SCIENCE AND HEALTH WITH
KEY TO THE SCRIPTURES," be given therefor, or unless
at the written request of Mrs. Eddy the Executive Members
of The First Church of Christ, Scientist, (formally called
the "First Members,") by a two-thirds vote of all their
number, decide so to do. And that the same inscription
which is on the outside of the present church edifice shall
be placed on any new church erected on said lot. And in
consideration of one dollar to me paid by said Ira O.
Knapp, William B. Johnson, Joseph Armstrong and
Stephen A. Chase, the receipt whereof is hereby
acknowledged, I do hereby confirm the deed as above
mentioned, and do grant and release unto them, their heirs,
successors and assigns in trust as aforesaid, the premises
therein described.

In Witness Whereof I have hereunto set my hand and seal
this nineteenth day of March, A. D. nineteen hundred and
three.

ALBERT METCALF. [Seal]

COMMONWEALTH OF MASSACHUSETTS

SUFFOLK March 20th, 1903

Then said Albert Metcalf acknowledged the foregoing instrument to be his free act and deed.

Before me

MALCOLM McLOUD.

Justice of the Peace.

March 20, 1903. at twelve o'clock and sixteen minutes P.M.

Received, Entered and Examined.

Attest: THOS. F. TEMPLE, Reg.

A true copy from the RECORDS OF DEEDS for the COUNTY OF SUFFOLK, Lib. 2886, Fol. 521.

Attest: CHAS. W. KIMBALL, Asst. Reg.

Made in the USA
Middletown, DE
11 May 2022

65630152R00055

Manual of The Mother Church

The First Church of Christ Scientist In Boston,
Massachusetts

by Mary Bakcr Eddy

Discoverer and founder of Christian Science

And author of Science and Health with

Key to the Scriptures

Originally published in 1895.